www.raintreepublishers.co.uk
Visit our website to find out
more information about
Raintree books.

To order:
☎ Phone 0845 6044371
🖹 Fax +44 (0) 1865 312263
💻 Email myorders@raintreepublishers.co.uk

Customers from outside the UK please telephone +44 1865 312262

Raintree is an imprint of Capstone Global Library Limited,
a company incorporated in England and Wales having its
registered office at 7 Pilgrim Street, London, EC4V 6LB –
Registered company number: 6695582

Text © Capstone Global Library Limited 2012
First published in hardback in 2012
The moral rights of the proprietor have been asserted.

All rights reserved. No part of this publication may be
reproduced in any form or by any means (including
photocopying or storing it in any medium by electronic
means and whether or not transiently or incidentally to
some other use of this publication) without the written
permission of the copyright owner, except In accord-
ance with the provisions of the Copyright, Designs and
Patents Act 1988 or under the terms of a licence issued
by the Copyright Licensing Agency, Saffron House,
6¬–10 Kirby Street, London EC1N 8TS (www.cla.co.uk).
Applications for the copyright owner's written permission should be addressed to the publisher.

Edited by Adam Miller, Andrew Farrow, and
 Adrian Vigliano
Designed by Philippa Jenkins
Original illustrations © Capstone Global Library
 Limited 2011
Illustrated by Terry Pastor / www.theartagency.co.uk
Picture research by Mica Brancic
Originated by Capstone Global Library Ltd
Printed and bound in China by CTPS

ISBN 978 1 406 23387 2 (hardback)
15 14 13 12
10 9 8 7 6 5 4 3 2

British Library Cataloguing in Publication Data
Claybourne, Anna.
What are the limits of organ transplantation?. -- (Sci-hi)
617.9'54-dc22
A full catalogue record for this book is available from the
British Library.

Acknowledgments
The author and publishers are grateful to the following
for permission to reproduce copyright material: Corbis
pp. 7 (© Bettmann), 17 (© Mediscan), 19 (Science
Faction/© Centers for Disease Control - digital version
copyright Science Faction/James Gathaney), 23 (©
Reuters/Bazuki Muhammad), 24 (© David Howells),
28 (Reuters/© Pascal Rossignol), 32 (Reuters/© Benoit
Tessier), 33 (National Geographic Society/© Mark
Thiessen), 10 to 11 (© Bettmann); Getty Images p. 20
(Photographer's Choice RF/David Joel); Reuters p. 35
(© Ho New); Science Photo Library pp. 9 (Peter Arnold
Inc./Michelle Del Guercio), 12 (Klaus Guldbrandsen), 14
(LIfe In VIew), 26 (Reporters/John Thys), 30 (Anatomical
Travelogue), 36 (Bodenham, LTH NHS Trust), 39 (Massimo
Brega, The Lighthouse), 41, 5 top (Michelle Del Guercio);
Shutterstock pp. 27 middle and bottom (© Anat-oli), 27
top (© Yuri Arcurs), Contents page bottom (© Jeff Banke),
Contents page top (© Anat-oli). All background design
feature pictures courtesy of Shutterstock.

Main cover photograph of a heart transplant reproduced
with permission of Alamy (© mauritius images GmbH);
inset cover photograph of a human eye for cornea
harvesting reproduced with permission of Science Photo
Library (Massimo Brega, The Lighthouse).

The publisher would like to thank literary consultant
Nancy Harris and content consultant Ann Fullick for their
assistance in the preparation of this book.

Every effort has been made to contact copyright holders
of material reproduced in this book. Any omissions will
be rectified in subsequent printings if notice is given to
the publisher.

Disclaimer
All the Internet addresses (URLs) given in this book were
valid at the time of going to press. However, due to the
dynamic nature of the Internet, some addresses may
have changed, or sites may have changed or ceased to
exist since publication. While the author and publisher
regret any inconvenience this may cause readers, no
responsibility for any such changes can be accepted by
either the author or the publisher.

Contents

How could a pig save your life?

Find out on page 26!

How long does heart transplant surgery take?

Turn to page 10 to find out!

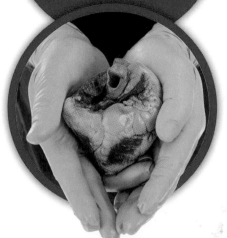

Some words are shown in bold, **like this**. These words are explained in the glossary. You will find important information and definitions underlined, <u>like this</u>.

NEW for OLD

Our bodies are amazing organisms. They're made up of thousands of working parts, which do all the jobs that keep us alive. But what if an important body part stops working? Amazingly, many body parts can be completely replaced, by **transplanting** (putting in) new ones.

WHAT IS AN ORGAN?

An **organ** is a body part that does a particular job to keep the body working. The heart is one example. Its job is to pump blood around your body all the time, day and night. Your blood carries **oxygen** and food to all the **cells** (building blocks of living things) that make up your body. Without these, the cells could not work.

ORGAN TRANSPLANTATION

If something goes wrong with an organ, it can cause serious health problems. Most of the time, medicines or other treatments can keep a patient well. But sometimes the best cure is to have an **organ transplant**. This is when doctors replace an unhealthy organ with a healthy one.

Thousands of organ transplants take place around the world each year. However, there are various problems that make organ transplantation difficult and complicated. This book explores these issues, and discusses how they affect the organ transplants we can do. These topics include:

- Where do new organs come from?
- Who should be first in line for an organ?
- Will the patient's body accept a new organ?
- Will the patient survive the risky operation?
- Are transplant operations worth the high cost?
- Is organ transplantation right or wrong?

All these things limit how many transplants can take place, the kinds of transplants we can do, and the people who can have them.

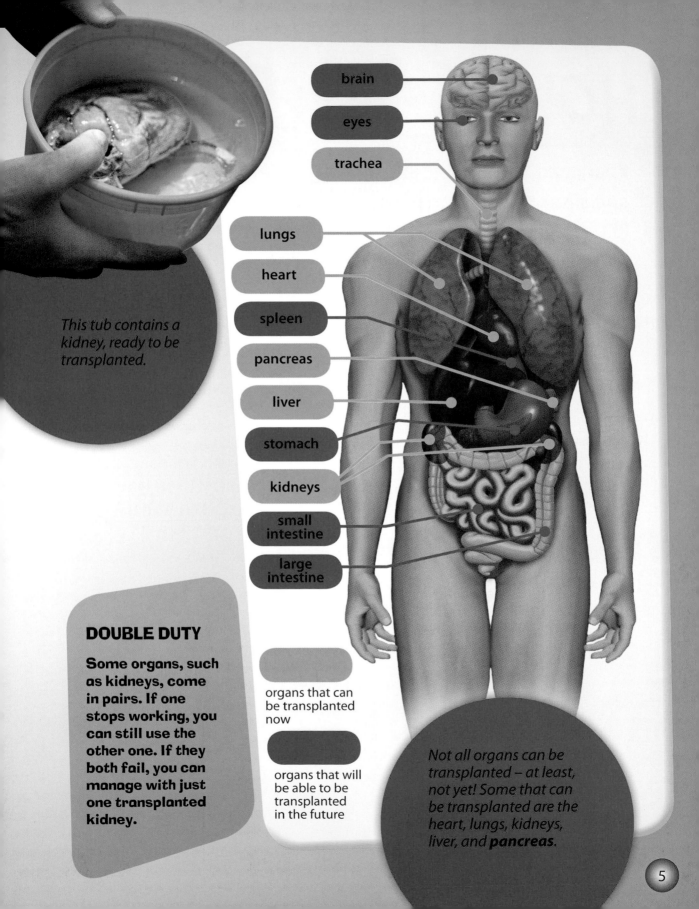

brain

eyes

trachea

lungs

heart

spleen

pancreas

liver

stomach

kidneys

small intestine

large intestine

This tub contains a kidney, ready to be transplanted.

DOUBLE DUTY

Some organs, such as kidneys, come in pairs. If one stops working, you can still use the other one. If they both fail, you can manage with just one transplanted kidney.

organs that can be transplanted now

organs that will be able to be transplanted in the future

*Not all organs can be transplanted – at least, not yet! Some that can be transplanted are the heart, lungs, kidneys, liver, and **pancreas**.*

HOW IT ALL BEGAN

Simple replacement body parts, such as wooden legs and silver hands, date from ancient times. But when early scientists tried swapping **organs** or blood between humans, it didn't work. The patient usually died.

TRANSPLANT PIONEERS

In the early 1900s, a French doctor, Alexis Carrel, figured out a way to sew together **blood vessels**, which are the tubes that carry blood throughout the body. **Transplanted** organs could now be fully connected to the new owner. Carrel also worked on keeping organs alive outside the body, ready for transplantation.

Starting in the 1930s, a Russian scientist, Vladimir Demikhov, carried out amazing transplant experiments on animals. They included heart and lung transplants in dogs. He even tried to give a dog a head transplant. The animals didn't live long, and some people might say it was wrong for Demikhov to test his ideas on animals this way. However, his work helped pave the way for human **organ transplants**.

Twin transplant

In 1954, US doctor Joseph Murray transplanted a kidney from one man to his identical twin brother. Because the men were twins their genes were identical. Genes give cells instructions that tell them what to do. Because their genes were identical the patient's body did not recognize the new kidney as different from his own, and did not reject it. The operation saved the man's life.

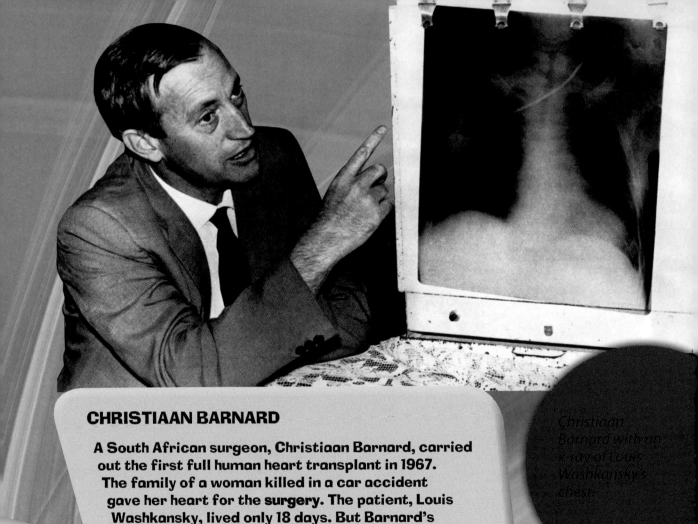

Christiaan Barnard with an x-ray of Louis Washkansky's chest.

CHRISTIAAN BARNARD

A South African surgeon, Christiaan Barnard, carried out the first full human heart transplant in 1967. The family of a woman killed in a car accident gave her heart for the surgery. The patient, Louis Washkansky, lived only 18 days. But Barnard's work amazed the world, and led to today's more successful heart transplant operations.

ORGAN REJECTION

Through his experiments, Carrel discovered that the main problem with transplants was organ **rejection**. The body's **immune system,** which fights germs and diseases, reacts to transplanted organs as if the body were being invaded by harmful foreign **cells**. It tries to attack and get rid of them. When **surgeons** tried organ transplants in humans, the transplants almost always failed.

Then, in the 1960s, doctors began using drugs to **suppress**, or weaken, the immune system, so that the body did not fight the new organ. Gradually, these drugs got better and better, helping patients to live longer after transplants.

THE STORY OF A TRANSPLANT

1 Heart transplant patients

If someone has a damaged heart or serious heart disease, doctors do tests to see if he needs a **transplant**. He must be strong and fit enough to survive the operation.

2 On the waiting list

If a patient is suitable for a transplant, he is put on a waiting list for **donor** hearts.

3 An organ is found

No one knows exactly when and where a new heart will be ready. This only happens when someone dies, leaving a healthy heart to be donated.

4 Making a match

As soon as a heart is available, medical teams check the waiting list to find the best person to give it to. They consider who needs a heart most, who has **genes** that match the heart best, and how nearby the patient is.

5 Keeping it fresh

The heart is removed from the donor, and packed for transportation. It can be kept in a chilled liquid, or attached to a machine that pumps blood through it and keeps it beating.

This picture shows an old, damaged heart (on the right), and a device that helps a failing heart to pump blood. They are both removed when a new heart is transplanted.

DECIDING TO DONATE

When someone dies, her family may have to decide whether to donate her organs. Or, if the person has chosen to be a donor, the family has to let her organs be taken by the doctor. This can be very upsetting. Doctors have to be kind and sensitive to the relatives, while arranging for the person's organs to be used as quickly as possible.

6

Organ transport

The heart travels to its destination on a special organ transport van or plane. Meanwhile, a skilled team of **surgeons** and support staff have to be ready to swing into action.

Turn the page to find out what happens during the operation...

7

Ready for surgery

When the doctor is told that a donor heart is ready, the patient goes into an **operating theatre** for the operation. He lies on an operating table and is given **anesthesia** to put him to sleep and numb all pain.

8

The incision

The surgeon cuts open the patient's skin and cuts through the bones in his chest to reach the heart.

How long does it take?

A heart transplant operation takes from 4 to 6 hours. Other transplants can take more or less time.

Liver	5 – 8 hours
1 lung	4 – 8 hours
2 lungs	8 – 12 hours
Heart and lung	Up to 12 hours
Kidney	2 – 4 hours
Pancreas	Around 3 hours

SURVIVAL RATES

Of patients having a heart transplant, 80 to 90 percent will still be alive one year later. This figure is gradually rising as new and better surgical techniques are introduced.

9

Pumping machine

While the heart is being replaced, the patient is connected to a **heart bypass machine**. It takes over the job of pumping blood throughout the body.

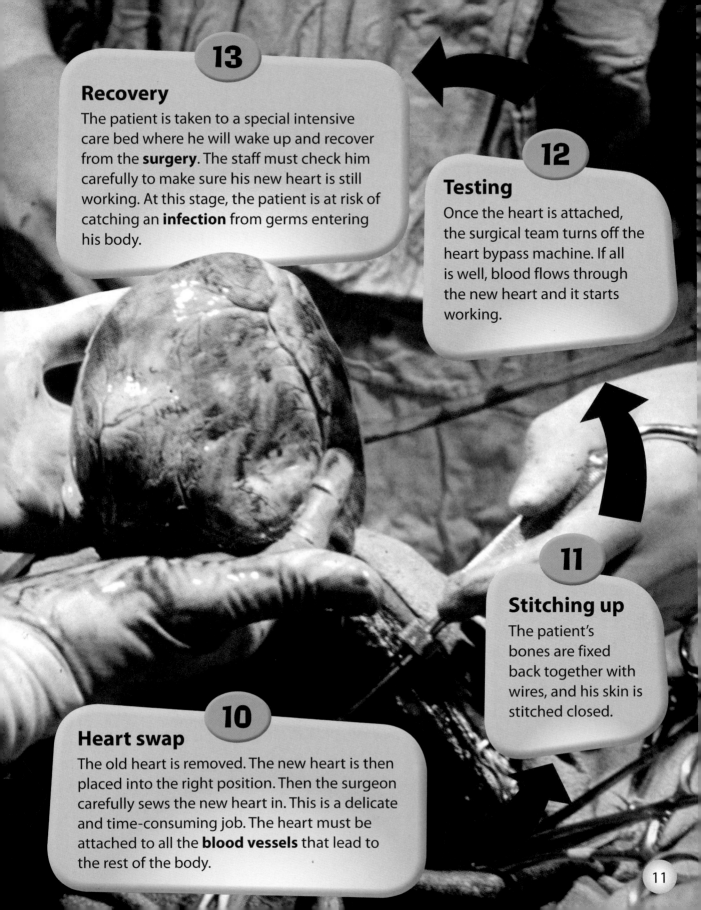

13 Recovery

The patient is taken to a special intensive care bed where he will wake up and recover from the **surgery**. The staff must check him carefully to make sure his new heart is still working. At this stage, the patient is at risk of catching an **infection** from germs entering his body.

12 Testing

Once the heart is attached, the surgical team turns off the heart bypass machine. If all is well, blood flows through the new heart and it starts working.

11 Stitching up

The patient's bones are fixed back together with wires, and his skin is stitched closed.

10 Heart swap

The old heart is removed. The new heart is then placed into the right position. Then the surgeon carefully sews the new heart in. This is a delicate and time-consuming job. The heart must be attached to all the **blood vessels** that lead to the rest of the body.

KIDNEY TRANSPLANTS

The kidney is the organ most commonly transplanted worldwide. There are more than 60,000 kidney transplant operations every year.

The kidneys filter waste out of your blood. Without them, poisons collect in your body. Luckily, a single transplanted kidney can do the job. Kidney failure is common, and a living donor can give up a kidney for transplant without much danger. People can donate a kidney to help a family member.

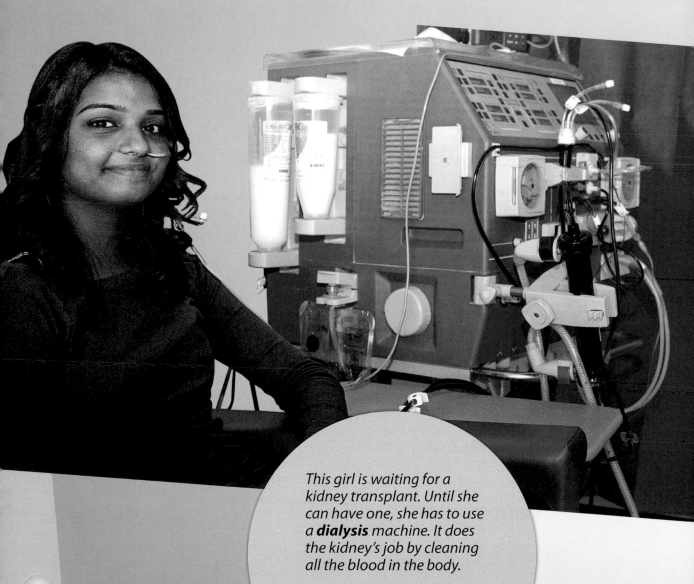

*This girl is waiting for a kidney transplant. Until she can have one, she has to use a **dialysis** machine. It does the kidney's job by cleaning all the blood in the body.*

LIVER TRANSPLANTS

The liver does a lot of jobs, including storing and making useful body substances. It took a long time to develop successful liver transplants, and they are still difficult and risky. But now, livers can be transplanted from donors who have died, or by using just a part of a living donor's liver. Amazingly, if you donate a section of your liver, it can **regenerate**, or regrow, itself in a few weeks. Most other organs cannot regrow like this.

PANCREAS

The **pancreas** is a small organ that makes **insulin**. Insulin is a chemical that keeps your blood healthy. **Diabetes** is a disease in which the pancreas makes too little insulin. People with severe diabetes sometimes need pancreas transplants. The operation is dangerous and difficult. But in 2010, surgeons tried a new method, using a robot to help do the **surgery**. The robot arms could work much more delicately and in more detail than human hands alone. They could also reach inside the patient's body to do the work through small cuts in the skin. This makes the operation safer, because the body doesn't need to be opened up.

Kidneys for sale

In some countries people sell kidneys for transplants, even though this is usually against the law. This can lead to all kinds of problems, such as unhealthy people selling a kidney in order to get money, and even people being murdered and having their kidneys stolen to be sold.

DID YOU KNOW?

When surgeons transplant a kidney, they don't usually take the damaged ones out. They just transplant the new one next to one of the other kidneys.

BODY BITS AND PIECES

Complex, dramatic transplants, such as heart and face transplants, hit the headlines more often than routine transplants. But smaller body parts are often transplanted, too. You might not even have heard of the **thymus** or **cornea**, but one day you, or someone you know, might need a new one.

Here are some of the lesser-known transplants:

Cornea	The clear front part of the eye. It can be damaged by diseases, causing blindness. The cornea is a **body tissue** (or material), not a true organ, and is relatively easy to transplant.
Small intestine	A tube that absorbs food chemicals. A transplant helps people whose small intestine is damaged, or too short.
Bone marrow	Soft tissue inside the bones that makes blood cells. Some types of cancer can be cured with a transplant of bone marrow from a living donor.
Heart valve	A flap inside the heart that opens and closes to let blood through. Faulty valves can be replaced by valves taken from pigs or cows. They can also be replaced by artificial or fake valves.

Gift of life

It can be very hard to decide whether to become a living donor. People often want to help a friend or family member, or even a stranger. They may donate a kidney, bone marrow, or a section of lung or liver. But donating means having an operation, which can be dangerous. Losing body parts can sometimes make donors sick, too. Would you give up a body part to help someone else?

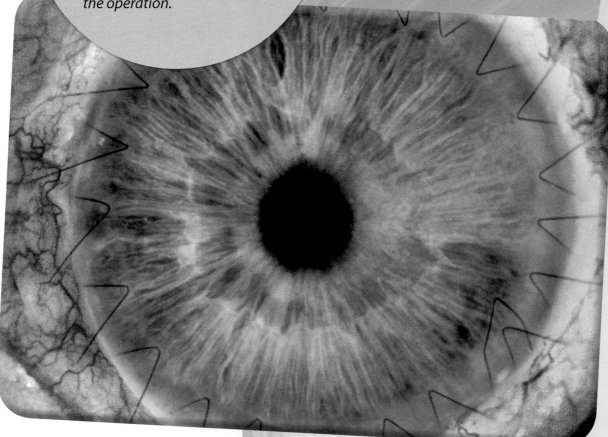

A close-up photo of an eye with a newly transplanted cornea. You can see the stitches holding the new cornea in place. They are removed about a year after the operation.

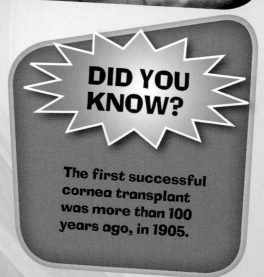

DID YOU KNOW?

The first successful cornea transplant was more than 100 years ago, in 1905.

THE PROBLEM OF REJECTION

Organs are precious, so doctors try as hard as they can to stop the patient's **immune system** from **rejecting** and attacking them.

A GOOD MATCH

To help avoid rejection, the **donor** and the patient should be a good **genetic** match. This includes:

- Having the same **blood group**, or type of blood

- Having **antigens** which are as similar as possible. Antigens are special molecules found on **cell** surfaces and everyone (except identical twins) has their own unique set. Antigens are recognized by the immune system.

- For some **transplants**, matching the donor's and patient's ages also helps

- Having similar **DNA** (a chemical found inside cells and that **genes** are made of).

If rejection happens, the patient will get a **fever**, or high temperature. The patient usually feels very tired, and if the rejection is very bad the new organ will stop working. Some rejection is very common after a transplant. It can be treated with medicines, but sometimes it's so serious that the patient needs another transplant.

Fascinating fact

One Australian liver transplant patient, Demi-Lee Brennan, does not need anti-rejection drugs at all. When her new liver was transplanted in 2001, it wasn't a very good match. But instead of being rejected, it took over, and changed her blood type to match its own. Brennan is the only person this has happened to so far, and she's still healthy. Doctors are studying her to see if they could make it happen in other patients.

AVOIDING ILLNESS

Because of the risk of rejection, transplant patients usually have to take drugs to **suppress** their immune systems for the rest of their lives. This means their bodies are not as good at fighting germs. To stay healthy, they may have to:

- Avoid cuts and scrapes

- Stay away from people with colds and flu

- Keep their hands clean and germ-free

- Keep their teeth very clean

- Avoid pets, soil, and dirt, as they could carry germs

If transplant patients do get infected with germs, they may have to go to the hospital for more treatment. This is because their bodies cannot fight the germs off on their own.

Colds and flu make people sneeze. This spreads germs out into the air and other people can easily breathe them in. That's why transplant patients have to stay away from people who are sick.

ORGAN DONATION

Organ transplants depend on a supply of **organs**. For most **transplants**, these can only come from other people, called **organ donors**.

ORGAN SHORTAGE

Getting enough organs and deciding how to distribute them are big problems for transplant doctors and patients. There are always more patients waiting for an organ than there are organs available. Some people wait years for a **donor** organ, and others die from their illness before an organ is found.

DONATING AFTER DEATH

Some organs can come from living donors, but most are taken when someone dies. If a person dies while he is fit and healthy, for example in an accident, his organs can often help several patients. His heart, lungs, liver, and kidneys could all be transplanted. But for this to happen, he or his family has to agree to it.

WILLING TO DONATE

To avoid having relatives decide about donating a family member's organs, many people carry a **donor card**. It says the person is willing to donate his or her organs. People can also sign up on a **donor register**, which is a list of people who have agreed to donate. With these documents, doctors can check quickly and easily if they can take a person's organs.

WHAT WOULD YOU DO?

It seems to make sense to decide to donate your organs, if it could help others. Yet a lot of people don't like the idea of their organs being removed after they die. On the other hand, it often helps families to know that although their relative has died, he or she can still help someone else. What do you think? Would you carry a donor card or register as a donor?

Donor Card

I would like to help someone to live after my death.

READY TO GO

Once an organ is donated, doctors can match it to the best recipient, and send it off to be transplanted. Usually, they check a list of people waiting for organs in the same area or country. If they can't make a good match there, the organ might be offered to neighbouring countries to see if they have a suitable recipient for it. The organ can't travel too far, though, because it will only stay in good condition for a few hours.

WHO GETS THE ORGANS?

Every organ should go to whoever needs it most and matches it best. But it's not always that simple. There are many reasons why some people get organs and others don't.

Firstly, although it's usually against the law, many people get organs, especially kidneys, by paying for them (see page 15). Most governments try to combat illegal trade in organs, but it's hard to stop it completely, because it usually happens secretly.

Secondly, in some countries, such as the United States, some people have **medical insurance** to pay for hospital treatment, and others don't. Also, some people have better insurance plans than others. For example, because poor people are less likely to have a good insurance plan, they may be less likely to get an organ transplant.

Usually, doctors are not allowed to choose who gets an organ based on a person's age or lifestyle. But they may decide that someone who is healthier will benefit more from a new organ than someone who is less healthy. So being very old, or having a body damaged by smoking or drinking, for example, could place a person further down on the patient list.

Picking and choosing

Some people want to donate organs only if they can choose who receives them, such as people of a particular race or religion. This is not allowed. Once the organ is donated, the medical team decides how it is used.

YOU DECIDE

Who do you think should have a donor organ?

- An older person who has waited a long time for a transplant, or a young child?

- A healthy person who has never smoked, or someone who needs a transplant because smoking has damaged his organs?

- Someone who can pay a lot of money for an organ, or someone who can't pay anything and so will be expensive to treat?

AT THE CUTTING EDGE

Heart and kidney **transplants** are very common now. But some types of transplants are still new. They have only just started being used on humans.

This baby was born after her mother had an ovary removed, then re-transplanted after cancer treatment.

OVARY TRANSPLANT

The two **ovaries** are **organs** that only women have. They release **egg cells** that can join with male **sperm cells** to grow into a baby. To have a baby, a woman needs at least one working ovary. But ovaries can stop working, especially as a **side effect** of treatment for cancer.

An ovary transplant can help a woman have a baby, but anti-rejection drugs can also stop ovaries from working. Because of this, transplants have only worked for women who have had an ovary donated by an identical twin. Identical twins have **genes** that match, so there's no **rejection** of the organ and the anti-rejection drugs aren't needed (see page 7). However, such transplants are rare.

SAVED IN THE FREEZER

If a woman knows she is going to have cancer treatments that will damage her ovaries, there's a new method she can use to save tissue from her healthy ovaries:

- Doctors take some **cells** from one of the patient's ovaries and freeze them.

- After the cancer treatment, doctors transplant the tissue back into the patient's ovaries.

- The transplanted tissue makes the damaged ovary start working and releasing eggs again.

- The patient does not reject the transplant, because it consists of her own **body tissue**.

WOMB TRANSPLANT

Doctors are now working on a **womb**, or **uterus**, transplant, too, though it's still at an experimental stage. The womb is the organ that holds a baby as it grows. Women don't need a womb to stay alive, so wombs could come from living **donors**. The wombs could also be removed from the patient when they're no longer needed. Some women have their womb removed for medical reasons, so they might be able to provide the donor organs.

ANIMAL PARTS

Before **organ transplants** became common in humans, scientists such as Vladimir Demikhov (see page 6) experimented on animals. Scientists still try out new transplant methods in animals before using them in humans. But animals could soon play an even bigger role. We already take heart **valves** from pigs. We **modify**, or make changes, to them, and transplant them into humans (see page 16). One day, animals could provide most other organs, too, using new methods that are still being developed. But how would that work?

GENETIC ENGINEERING

Genetic engineering means changing the genes of a living organism. Genes are the instructions inside cells that control how a living being grows and works. Genes are made from **DNA**. Scientists can change an animal's genes by cutting up sections of DNA and adding new DNA taken from another **species** (type of living thing).

Eventually, people might be able use genetic engineering to make an animal such as a pig grow humanlike organs or tissues. We might even be able to change the DNA to match a particular transplant patient and avoid rejection.

Is using animals wrong?

Would you think it was okay to have an organ grown especially for you in a pig or another animal? Do you think that breeding and killing an animal for its organs is different from using animals for meat, or the same thing?

Pigs could be used to grow organs for transplant, as their bodies are similar to ours in several ways.

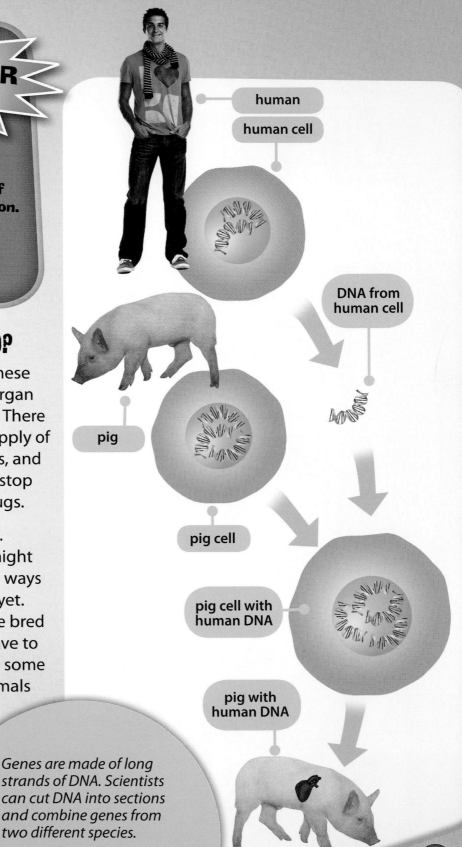

WILL IT EVER HAPPEN?

We are constantly pushing the limits of organ transplantation. Where will it stop? Can you think of an organ that could not be transplanted?

THE WAY AHEAD?

Some scientists think these methods could make organ transplants hassle-free. There would be a plentiful supply of healthy, suitable organs, and organ recipients could stop using anti-rejection drugs.

But there are problems. Organs from animals might give people diseases in ways we haven't thought of yet. The animals couldn't be bred on farms, but would have to live in special labs. And some people think using animals in this way is morally wrong.

Genes are made of long strands of DNA. Scientists can cut DNA into sections and combine genes from two different species.

human

human cell

DNA from human cell

pig

pig cell

pig cell with human DNA

pig with human DNA

BEYOND ORGANS

Did you know it's possible to have a new hand attached to your arm, and that it can work just like the old one did? Even more amazing, it's now possible to have a face **transplant**! These aren't true **organs**, but they are important. Transplanting them can transform patients' lives.

A stranger's face

One problem with face transplants is that the patient might feel strange about having someone else's appearance. Can you imagine what it would be like? What if you were related to the donor, and saw his or her face on someone else?

Isabelle Dinoire, the world's first face transplant patient, shown in 2006 after recovering from her operation.

A NEW FACE

Having your face seriously damaged is horrific. People don't need a face to live, but our faces are a huge part of who we are. Doctors can now replace a face that's been badly burned or injured, with a face from a **donor** who has died.

Surgeons have to attach the **blood vessels**, **nerves** (**cells** that carry signals to and from the brain), and other parts in the donor face to the patient. This gives the new face blood flow, feeling, and movement. The new face usually looks like a mixture of the donor and the patient, as it changes shape when attached to the patient's head. It doesn't always look perfect, but is a big improvement over the damaged face the patient had before. The operation is so complicated, it can take up to 24 hours to complete.

OSCAR

A Spanish farmer known as Oscar had the first complete (rather than just partial) face transplant in 2010. His face had been destroyed in a shooting accident.

HAND TRANSPLANTS

Like a face, a hand is tricky to transplant, because of its fine, detailed movements. Some early attempts at hand transplants, in the 1990s, did not succeed. But now dozens of people have had one or both hands replaced after accidents, using real human hands from dead donors.

To make sure a transplanted hand works properly everything has to be connected, including the nerves and the blood vessels.

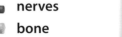

blood vessels

nerves

bone

TRACHEA TRANSPLANT

The **trachea**, or **windpipe**, is the tube that carries air between the mouth and lungs. It's an important organ, because you need it in order to breathe. Some babies are born with a trachea that's too narrow. Some people have their trachea damaged by diseases or accidents. All these problems can be cured with a transplant.

In this diagram you can see clearly how the trachea carries air into all parts of the lungs.

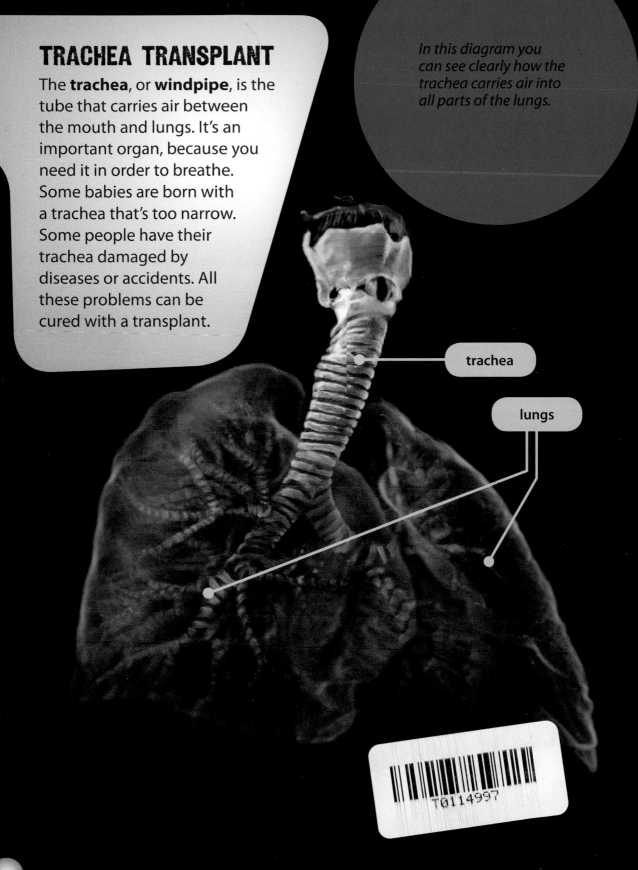

trachea

lungs

STEM CELL METHOD

Until 2008, trachea transplants had only been tried on animals such as pigs. But now several people have had these transplants, using a groundbreaking method. The doctors take a trachea from a donor who has died, and then remove cells from it. This leaves just the framework, a bit like a skeleton. As it has no cells, and therefore no **DNA**, it will not be **rejected**.

Then healthy trachea cells from the patient's own body are added to the framework, along with **stem cells** from the patient's own body. Stem cells from an adult are body cells which can grow into several different types of cells.

The stem cells become new trachea cells that cover the framework. The trachea is then transplanted without the problem of rejection. This is because the trachea's DNA comes from the patient herself. This method is st early stages, but has been shown to work in patie

CIARAN FINN-LYNCH

In 2010, an 11-year-old British boy, Ciaran Finn-Lynch, became the first child to have a trachea transplant. The new trachea replaced his damaged trachea, which was only 1 millimetre wide. A healthy trachea is around 20 millimetres wide.

Where is it from?

Transplants are given different names depending on where the donated organ or tissue comes from.

Autografts	From your own body
Allografts	From another person
Isografts	From someone whose DNA matches yours exactly, such as an identical twin
Xenografts	From a different species, such as a pig

ARTIFICIAL ORGANS

Finding **organ donors** and working to avoid organ **rejection** are very difficult jobs. One way to make the **organ transplant** process easier is to build artificial **organs**, or other body parts, from scratch.

Some of the components of an artificial heart being developed for use in human beings.

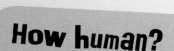

How human?

In science fiction stories, a **cyborg** is a being that is part biological or natural, and part machine or robot. So if you had a feeling, moving robotic hand, or an artificial (fake) heart, that would make you a cyborg! How much of you would have to be artificial before you were no longer human?

ARTIFICIAL HEARTS

The heart is a pump that pushes blood throughout the body. Machines that can do this job were first used in the 1950s, and are still used today. But they're big and bulky, and work outside the patient's body, connected by tubes.

Over the years, though, doctors and scientists have developed smaller artificial hearts that can be implanted inside the chest. But there have been problems with them, which need to be solved. Some are how to power the heart, how to make it beat faster when needed, and how to stop it from clogging up. The latest designs might eventually be able to replace heart **transplants**. After testing, they could be available by around 2015. Using artificial hearts should avoid rejection problems, because they would not contain living **cells** from another person.

BIONIC BODY PARTS

You might think that working robotic hands and limbs belong in science fiction stories. In fact, they're real. Scientists have invented **prosthetic**, or fake, robot hands that can be attached to the **nerves** in a patient's arm. The patient's brain can send signals to the hand to move it. Some hands have a sense of touch, too. They can sense or detect when something presses on the surface of the fingers, and can send messages back to the patient's brain along their own nerves.

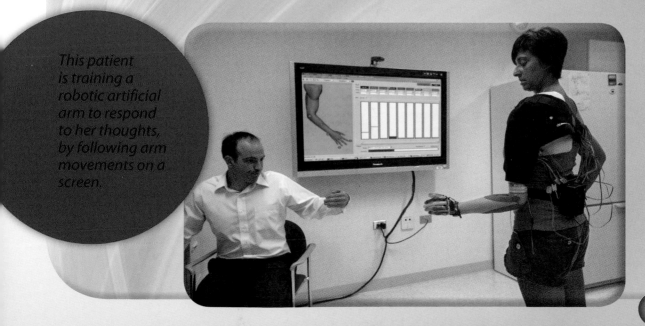

This patient is training a robotic artificial arm to respond to her thoughts, by following arm movements on a screen.

THE INCREDIBLE EAR MOUSE

In 1996 an amazing image hit the headlines. The picture showed a mouse with a human ear growing on its back. Or did it? Many people thought that the mouse had been **genetically engineered** (see page 26). They thought it contained human **genes**, making it grow a human ear.

In fact, the ear was not human at all. It was artificial, and was made by covering an ear-shaped object made from polyester fabric with **cartilage** from a cow. Cartilage is the tough, flexible substance ears are made from. The ear structure was placed under the mouse's skin. As a living animal, its blood supply fed the cartilage cells, and they grew and covered the ear.

SPARE EARS

US scientists Dr. Charles Vacanti and Dr. Linda Griffith-Cima were behind the ear mouse experiment. It was a way of making artificial body parts, such as ears and noses, which could be transplanted onto patients who had lost theirs. These simple parts were just for appearance, and could not actually work. For example, the mouse could not hear through the ear. But similar methods are now being used to make other, working body parts, such as artificial **bladders**. A bladder is the body part that holds urine.

Headline horror

The ear mouse caused great controversy around the world. People were shocked and horrified to think that scientists were combining human and mouse genes to make an ear-backed monster. In fact, this was not true at all, but the misleading and incorrect news stories caused panic. This is an example of how news stories don't always tell the whole truth! With controversial science stories like this, it's important to check the evidence and find out what really happened.

A reporter looks at the ear mouse. The mouse was a special kind that had no fur, so that it would grow a more normal-looking human ear.

WHAT ARE THE ETHICAL LIMITS?

Organ transplantation is complicated. It involves cutting-edge science, detailed operations, and major dangers. It also involves a lot of people, upsetting situations, and extreme emotions. The **ethics**, or rights and wrongs, of the process are complex, too. Some people think all **organ** transplantation is wrong. Others have concerns about some aspects or parts of it.

WHAT IF YOU WERE ILL?

What if you needed an organ transplant to save your life? Would you change your mind about any of your views?

If you were seriously ill, you might have to stay in a hospital permanently. You might depend on machines to keep you alive. An organ transplant might be able to give you a normal life again.

What do you think about these issues?

Is it right to swap and share body parts? Some people think you should not cut up a dead body, or add one person's body part to someone else.

Should people be allowed to donate organs while they're still alive? In their eagerness to help a relative, they could harm themselves. Or they could feel pressured into giving up their organ.

Is organ donation unfair? With a shortage of organs, someone is always going to benefit, and someone else isn't. How can we determine who deserves a second chance the most?

Should people be given a **transplant** organ if they've made themselves ill, for example by smoking? What if they were injured while doing a dangerous sport like skydiving?

Should buying and selling organs remain illegal, or should it be allowed? Should you be allowed to sell your own kidney if you want to?

Is it better or worse to take organs from animals instead of people? Should animals be raised in labs for this purpose?

Should we spend money on organ transplants that might help someone live a few years, when it costs less to save more lives with vaccines, mosquito nets, or water and food aid?

37

OPT IN OR OPT OUT?

In some countries, such as the United States and United Kingdom, if people want to donate their organs, they have to say so. They carry a **donor card**, sign up on a **donor register** (see page 21), or let their relatives know their wishes. This is known as an opt in system.

But in other countries, such as Spain, there's an opt out system instead. There, doctors can transplant people's organs after death, unless they have opted out by saying they *don't* want to be a **donor**. In some cases, the doctors may also consult the family to make sure they agree, too.

WHICH IS BETTER?

An opt in system gives people more freedom. But an opt out system should make it easier to collect organs. However, some countries with an opt out system, such as Sweden, have lower donation rates than other countries with an opt in system, such as the United Kingdom. This is partly because organ donation depends on many factors, such as hospital facilities, and people's thoughts and beliefs. Would you prefer an opt in or opt out system?

FEELING GUILTY?

When someone has had a lifesaving organ transplant from a donor who has died, she sometimes feels guilty and sad that she is alive as a result of someone else's death. When people are waiting for a transplant, it can be even harder, because they know they are waiting for someone to die, probably in an accident. But if someone is gravely injured in an accident, isn't it best if some good comes of it by someone else's life being saved? Would you feel guilty in this circumstance?

This human cornea has been taken from the eye of a donor who has died. It is now ready to be used in a cornea transplant.

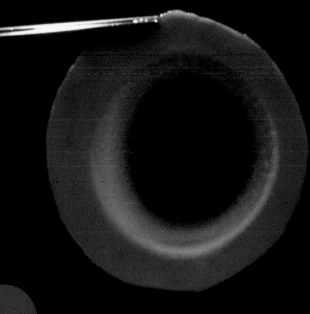

Not my eyes!

A lot of people agree to donate most of their organs, but not their eyes. If it weren't for this, more people could have their sight saved by cornea transplants. Yet many people still feel that their eyes are too personal to give away. Do you feel the same way?

FUTURE TRANSPLANTS

What will organ donation be like 5, 10, 20, or even 50 years from now?

BETTER AND BETTER

Well, it will probably get easier. Ways of collecting, moving, and **transplanting** organs are always improving. New medicines are keeping transplant patients alive for longer. And people may become more willing to donate organs, too.

But one day, we might not need **organ donors** at all. Scientists are looking for more ways to build new organs from body **cells**. And as microscale **nanotechnology** develops, we might be able to construct the tiny parts that make real organs work. We could then build more complex artificial organs, besides hearts.

STEM CELLS

Stem cells probably hold the most exciting possibilities. These cells can become any type of body cell (see page 31).

Because they can become any type of cell, stem cells could be used to grow any type of organ. To make it match the patient's **DNA**, the cells can be taken from the patient's own body.

CLONING

Scientists can copy someone's DNA and use it to grow an **embryo** (a group of cells in the early stages of becoming a baby). The embryo would be an exact genetic copy of that person. That is a **clone**. A cloned embryo could provide useful matching stem cells. Scientists hope that they will soon be able to grow whole new organs from cloned stem cells.

EMBRYO ETHICS

Using cells from embryos in research to try and grow new organs is carefully controlled by law. Some people think it is wrong to create an embryo as a medical cure. Many others think this is justified because new stem cell treatments could save hundreds of thousands of lives.

What is nanotechnology?

Nanotechnology means technology and engineering (designing and building things) on a tiny scale. It is still at an early stage, but eventually we could use it to build from scratch any object, even very complex ones such as human organs. Alternatively, nanotechnology machines could be sent into the body to rebuild and repair existing damaged organs. Perhaps nanotechnology will make organ transplants a thing of the past!

Stem cells shown under a microscope. These stem cells are ready to turn into blood cells.

TIMELINE

1900
Karl Landsteiner discovers **blood groups**

1902
Alexis Carrel develops method for stitching **blood vessels** together

1905
First successful **cornea** transplant

1910
Alexis Carrel discovers **rejection** of **organ transplants**

1960
First kidney transplant from a living **donor**

1959
First successful kidney transplant between nonidentical twins

1959
Vladimir Demikhov carries out his famous dog head transplant experiment

1954
First successful kidney transplant is carried out between identical twins

1963
First successful lung transplant

1967
First successful liver transplant; first successful full human heart transplant

1971
Donor cards launched

1982
Jarvik 7 artificial heart works in a patient for several months

1981
Stem cells first extracted from mouse **embryos**

1981
First successful heart–lung transplant

1998
First successful hand transplant

2006
Cells from human adults reprogrammed to become stem cells

2008
First **trachea** transplant using a trachea built with stem cells

2010
Oscar, a Spanish farm worker, receives the first full face transplant

QUIZ

Can you remember the answers to these questions, or find them somewhere in this book?

1 Name three body organs.

2 Who carried out the world's first successful full human heart transplant in 1967?

3 What type of animal did Vladimir Demikhov give a head transplant to?

4 What is it called when the body attacks a transplanted organ?

5 What is the most commonly transplanted organ?

6 What body part from a pig can you have implanted into you?

7 Why did Oscar need a full face transplant in 2010?

8 If you have an autograft transplant, where does the transplanted body tissue come from?

9 What type of artificial body part can have a sense of touch?

10 In 1995, did scientists create an eye mouse, an ear mouse, or a nose mouse?

Check the answers below to find your score out of 10.

Answers to Quiz: 1. Any of heart, lungs, liver, kidneys, pancreas, stomach, small intestine, large intestine, brain, eyes, ovary, thymus, womb, bladder. **2.** Christiaan Barnard. **3.** Dog. **4.** Rejection **5.** Kidney. **6.** Heart valve. **7.** His face was destroyed in a shooting accident. **8.** Your own body. **9.** Hand. **10.** Ear mouse.

Glossary

anesthesia drug that numbs pain or sends a person into a deep sleep

antigen chemical found on the surface of a cell which can be recognized by the immune system

bladder bag that stores urine inside the body

blood group one of several types of human blood

blood vessel tube that carries blood throughout the body

body tissue material the body is made of

bone marrow body tissue inside bones where blood cells are made

cartilage hard, flexible body tissue

cell tiny building block that living organisms are made of

clone exact copy of a living thing

cornea clear front part or "window" of the eye

cyborg creature that is part human, part machine

cystic fibrosis disease that clogs the lungs and other body parts

diabetes disease in which the body cannot make the important substance insulin

dialysis process of cleaning the body's blood when the kidneys have failed

DNA chemical found inside cells and that genes are made of

donor someone who donates, or gives, something such as an organ for transplant

donor card card that states a person is willing to donate organs after death

donor register list of people who are willing to donate organs after death

egg cell female sex cell which joins with a sperm cell to form a new individual

embryo group of cells in the early stages of becoming a baby

ethics system of morals or beliefs about what is right and wrong

fever raised body temperature

gene section of DNA that contains instructions for a living being

genetic relating to genes

genetic engineering changing a living organism's genes

heart bypass machine machine that can take over the heart's job of pumping blood

immune system body system which recognizes foreign cells and attacks the germs which cause disease

infection invasion of germs into the body

insulin body chemical that controls the amount of sugar in the blood

intestine tube that carries food or food waste through the body

medical insurance payments that allow you to have medical treatment if you need it

modify to change or alter something

nanotechnology technology involving microscopically small parts and machines

nerve cell that carries signals around the body and to and from the brain

operating theatre hospital room where operations are carried out

organ body part that does a particular job

organ donor someone who donates or gives one of his or her organs to be transplanted

organ transplant operation in which a faulty organ is replaced

ovary female organ that releases egg cells for making babies

oxygen gas found in the air that animals need to breathe

pancreas small organ that makes the body substance insulin

prosthetic replacement body part such as a hand, nose, or leg

regenerate rebuild or regrow

rejection process in which the body's immune system attacks a transplanted organ

side effect unintended effect of a medicine or drug

species type of living thing, or organism

sperm cell male body cell that can combine with an egg cell to make a new baby

stem cell cell that can become any particular type of body cell

suppress weaken or hold down

surgeon doctor who carries out operations or surgeries

surgery operation

thymus small organ that releases germ-fighting body cells

trachea breathing tube leading from the throat to the lungs

transplant take something from one place and install it in another

uterus strong, muscular female organ that holds a growing baby

valve structure which opens and closes to let blood through in one direction only

windpipe another name for the trachea

womb another name for the uterus

Books

Cells, Tissues, and Organs (The Human Machine) by Richard Spilsbury (Heinemann Library, 2008)

Organ Donation (Opposing Viewpoints) by Laura K. Egendorf (Greenhaven Press, 2009)

Organ Transplantation (Science at the Edge) by Ann Fullick (Heinemann Library, 2009)

Organ Transplantation (Science in the News) by Andrew Campbell (Franklin Watts, 2008)

Repairing and Replacing Organs (Why Science Matters) by Andrew Solway (Heinemann Library, 2009)

Websites

www.imss.org
Visit this International Museum of Surgical Science site for information on historical and modern surgery.

www.organdonor.gov
This official organ donation and transplant site has lots of questions and answers, facts, and details about particular transplant operations.

www.unos.org
This organ transplant network site has a lot of useful information.

www.transplantkids.co.uk
A kids' organ transplant website, with facts and real-life transplant stories.

www.wtgf.org
This is a website for the society that organizes an international sports contest for athletes who have had an organ transplant.

Topics to research

Donation survey

- Make a list of ethical debates, questions, and decisions relating to organ transplants. You can find several in this book to begin your list.
- Take a survey of friends and family to find out how they answer these questions or what their opinions are. For each person, find out if he or she would be willing to donate his or her own organs.
- What percentage of your sample would be organ donors?

Science projects

The three areas of science listed below all have an impact on organ transplantation, or could in the future. Can you find out more about each one?

Nanotechnology

Look for examples of nanotech machines and structures that have already been made.

Find out how nanotechnology could help build a copy of a natural object such as an organ.

Cloning

Find out about the history of how scientists learned to clone animals, such as Dolly the sheep.

What is the difference between reproductive cloning and therapeutic cloning?

Robotics

Find out about robots that are used to perform surgery. What kinds of operations can they help with?

Look for life stories of people who have had an arm, hand, or leg replaced with a robotic one.

Index